"All the President's Men and Women"

The Attorney General
through
Janet Reno

John Hamilton

Published by Abdo & Daughters, 4940 Viking Dr., Suite 622, Edina, MN 55435.

Library bound edition distributed by Rockbottom Books, Pentagon Tower, P.O. Box 36036, Minneapolis, Minnesota 55435.

Cover Photo by: Blackstar
Inside Photos by: The Bettmann Archive (8, 9, 15, 16, 17, 21, 23, 24, 26, 27)
AP/Wide World Photos (5, 20)

Edited By: Sue L. Hamilton

Library of Congress Cataloging–in–Publication Data
Hamilton, John, 1959-
    The Attorney General / written by John Hamilton.
        p.   cm — (All the President's men and women)
    Includes bibliographical references and index.
    ISBN 1-56239-251-4
    1. United States. Dept. of Justice. Office of the Attorney General—Juvenile literature.
2. Attorneys general—United States—Juvenile literature. 3. Attorneys general—United States—Biography—Juvenile literature. [1. United States Dept. of Justice Attorney General.]
I. Title. II. Series.
KF5107.H24   1993
353.5—dc20   93-1967
                                    CIP
                                      AC

Printed on Recycled Paper

CONTENTS

The President's Cabinet: An Overview 4

The Attorney General and the Justice Department 6

History of the Attorney General and the Justice Department 8

Organization of the Justice Department 10

      Antitrust..11

      Civil 12

      Civil Rights 12

      Criminal 12

      Land and Natural Resources 13

      Tax 13

The Bureaus 14

      Federal Bureau of Investigation (FBI) 14

      Bureau of Prisons 17

      United States Marshals Service 18

      Immigration and Naturalization Service 19

      Drug Enforcement Administration (DEA) 20

Biography: Janet Reno 21

Glossary 28

Connect With Books 31

Index 32

The President's Cabinet: An Overview

When someone is elected President of the United States, he (or she) immediately takes on a huge amount of responsibility. Presidents must oversee all laws passed by Congress. They're the head of the armed forces. They must decide foreign policy - how should the U.S. help its friends and allies, and how should we punish our enemies? If the economy stumbles, the President must try to get it back on the right track. Presidents must make sure that laws are handed down fairly; energy is used wisely; parks and other government lands are put to proper use; citizens are educated, put to work, and kept healthy. And that is just a small part of what Presidents do!

Obviously, no one person, no matter how smart, can possibly know everything there is to know to do a President's job. A President paints in broad strokes, deciding the tone and direction of how the country should be run. To help with the details, the President has a "cabinet," a group of people to meet with regularly for advice on important decisions that must be made every day.

There's no law that says the President must have a cabinet. It's a system that has evolved by custom over the years. The United States Constitution says that the President "may require the opinion, in writing, of the principal officer in each of the executive departments, upon any subject relating to the duties of their respective offices." But the President doesn't have to ask their advice, and doesn't have to go along with what they say if the President thinks they are wrong.

The heads of these cabinet departments are called "secretaries"and are appointed by the President. The Senate checks the secretarys' backgrounds and votes on whether to accept them. Nominees are picked for their experience and special talents in the areas they are to oversee. Only rarely is a President's pick rejected. After the Senate accepts, or "confirms" cabinet secretaries, the President alone has the right to remove them if unhappy with the way they are performing their duties.

When a President resigns, or is defeated in an election, the entire cabinet also resigns. New Presidents can rehire old cabinet members, but they usually want their own trusted advisers to help them run the country.

This book will focus on the **Attorney General**, the cabinet member who heads the Justice Department.

President Bill Clinton presides over his first Cabinet meeting in the Cabinet Room of the White House.

The Attorney General and the Justice Department

The Attorney General is the head lawyer for the United States. When legal advice is needed, the President turns to the Attorney General. The Attorney General is also chief of the Justice Department, which finds and prosecutes people who break Federal laws. (These are called laws of the land.) Prosecuting someone means finding evidence and bringing someone to court with the hope that a judge and jury will find the person guilty and send him or her to prison. The Justice Department is like a huge law firm whose clients are the citizens of the United States. By enforcing Federal laws, the Justice Department guards the Constitution and the rights of citizens protected under that document.

Breaking a Federal law means breaking a law that applies in all 50 states. It's a crime that affects not just individuals but the United States as a whole. People who break federal laws include kidnappers, traitors, spies, thieves who move stolen goods across state lines, or drug dealers who bring narcotics into this country. There are many other kinds of criminals who break Federal laws, so the Attorney General and his or her assistants in the Justice Department have a big job to do.

Specifically, the Justice Department plays the key role in protecting U.S. citizens against criminals and subversion, in ensuring healthy competition of business, in safeguarding the consumer, and in enforcing drug, immigration, and naturalization laws. The Justice Department also protects citizens through effective law enforcement, crime prevention, crime detection, and prosecution and rehabilitation of offenders. When a lawsuit comes up in the

Supreme Court in which the United States is involved, the Justice Department conducts that suit. It represents the United States Government in legal matters, and gives legal advice and opinions to the President and the heads of the other executive departments.

As head of the Justice Department, the Attorney General supervises all these activities, plus the activities of all the U.S. Attorneys and U.S. Marshals in the various districts around the country who help carry out Justice Department policy.

The Justice Department has many bureaus and divisions, and each one has a different task in seeing that federal laws are enforced and that justice is carried out equally across the land. This is a very big responsibility. Citizens of the U.S. have a right to expect that the Attorney General will enforce the law in a fair manner. Attorneys General and their staff of assistants, in addition to being legal experts, must have squeaky clean integrity so that citizens will respect their fairness in enforcing the law. Since the Attorney General is appointed by the President, it's the President's responsibility to choose someone with great legal expertise and integrity, not just political support.

For example, after President Nixon resigned because of the Watergate scandal in the 1970s, the integrity of the entire Justice Department was questioned. Many people thought that the Justice Department had tried to help President Nixon cover up the crimes committed during the scandal. To restore confidence in the department, Nixon's successor, President Ford, quickly appointed a legal scholar, Edward Levi, who had little to do with Washington, D.C., and politics. Confidence in the department was eventually restored.

Another example took place in 1993, when President Clinton nominated Zoë Baird to be his Attorney General. People thought Baird was a brilliant lawyer who would make a great Attorney General. But then a problem came to light: Baird had hired illegal immigrants as household workers and didn't

Zoë Baird

pay their social security taxes. At first glance, it might seem that this was a relatively minor offense. After all, barely one quarter of the people who hire household help pay their social security taxes. Nevertheless, citizens were outraged, and rightly so. Calls and letters poured into the President's office. How could the American people respect an Attorney General who didn't respect all the laws of the land, even if the law she broke was a small one? Baird was forced to withdraw her nomination.

The Attorneys General have an important and difficult job to do. Not only must they be experts in legal matters, but people must look up to them as an example. The law of the land is in the Attorney General's hands, and it must be handed down fairly and with integrity.

History of the Attorney General and the Justice Department

The first United States Attorney General, Edmund Jennings Randolph, was sworn in in 1789. Congress created the office of Attorney General because it knew the President, George Washington, would need legal advice. To create the office, Congress passed the Judiciary Act of 1789. This law also divided the United States into districts and set up courts in each one. In addition to the Attorney General, Congress created the job of U.S. Attorney, one for each district. U.S. Attorneys make sure the law is obeyed in their districts. The Attorney General oversees all the U.S. Attorneys.

Randolph was a close friend of Washington, both being natives of Virginia. Although Randolph was a full cabinet member, he had no real department to run. He simply advised Washington on legal matters when the President requested information. He also enforced Federal law with the help of a few assistants.

Edmund Jennings Randolph, first Attorney General of the United States.

This system of overseeing Federal law worked well for quite some time, even though the United States soon began expanding west. From the original 13 states, the country grew rapidly to include states stretching all the way to the Pacific Ocean. Naturally, the legal business of the government expanded as well. Finally, in 1870, after the Civil War, Congress decided that the Attorney General needed a department to help with the bigger workload, and the Justice Department was born. Although the official title is different than the other cabinet secretaries, the Attorney General is really the Secretary of Justice.

Today, in this complicated world, the Justice Department has expanded to include thousands of lawyers, investigators and agents, all of whom work for the Attorney General. Because the Attorney General has so much responsibility and oversees so many departments and people, his or her work is mainly administrative, meaning there's a lot of paperwork. But the Attorney General sets the tone for each Presidential Administration's approach to law enforcement. Some might want to emphasize a war on drugs and spend a great deal of the Justice Department's resources on combating the problem. Another Attorney General might decide that gang warfare is the biggest threat to American citizens, and spend resources in this area instead. Usually, the Justice Department splits its resources in a mix of ways, with some emphasis or highlight that reflects the President's goals.

Organization of the Justice Department

The Justice Department has many responsibilities and several departments, each with a different function and mission. The Attorney General decides, in broad strokes, the direction these departments should take. The heads of the different departments then figure out the details. These Assistant Attorneys General oversee the work of many lawyers who are specialists in the subject matter of their department.

It is the lawyers in each division who file lawsuits against criminals and argue their cases in the name of the United States. But just because they represent the United States doesn't mean they get any extra favor by judges and juries. If they can't prove their cases, they lose.

Antitrust

The Justice Department's Antitrust Division makes sure that monopolies and companies that restrain trade don't harm the American consumer. The first federal laws against monopolies were spelled out in the Sherman Antitrust Act of 1890. Prices in our society are normally set because of competition. If two companies sell the same product, people will usually buy from the company that sells it at the cheapest price. This is called market competition. A monopoly happens when there is only one seller of a product. Because of complete control over the item's supply, the seller can charge any price it wants on the product.

Monopolies can be created when several companies form a trust. As an example of a trust, imagine that video game cartridges are manufactured by 10 companies. Then imagine that these companies agree to get together and form a new, bigger company, and split the profits among them. This new company would be called a holding company, and would be run by a group of people called a board of trustees. This would be good for the 10 video game companies, because now there is no more competition. They can charge anything they want for cartridges. You, as a consumer, have two choices: pay the high prices, or go without video games.

Luckily, there are laws against this sort of thing, called Antitrust Laws. The Antitrust Division's task is to investigate whether monopolies exist, and to break them up by filing charges in court (sometimes called "trust busting"). It is the Antitrust Division's responsibility to be a watchdog for the American consumer, protecting them against unfair trade practices.

Civil

The Civil Division is probably the largest and most active division within the Justice Department. Its lawyers handle all civil lawsuits (as opposed to criminal lawsuits) involving the United States government.

Some of the kinds of lawsuits the Civil Division handles include fraud, patents, copyrights and trademarks. It also defends federal officers who have lawsuits brought against them in the course of their duties.

Civil Rights

Congress created the Justice Department's Civil Rights Division in 1957. The division's goal is to enforce federal laws forbidding discrimination against Americans because of race, color, sex, or religion. The areas it covers include voting, education, employment, housing, credit, and the use of public facilities. This means all Americans have the right to vote, a right to an education without discrimination, to open housing, to fair employment opportunities, and the right to use all public accommodations like bathrooms and parks.

When the Civil Rights Division finds that somebody's civil rights have been abused, it brings suit against the offenders in federal court. This is separate from any local laws that may have been violated. For example, in Los Angeles in 1992 several police officers were put on trial for beating motorist Rodney King. Even though they were found not guilty, they stood trial a second time in 1993 in federal court for violating King's civil rights. This time two of the officers were found guilty.

Criminal

When Congress passes criminal laws, it is up to the Justice Department's Criminal Division to enforce them. Federal criminal laws include many different types of offenses, including bank robbery, illegal gambling, cheating the government, mail fraud, bribery of public officials, and the illegal buying and selling of explosives, guns, and drugs.

The Criminal Division is also responsible for breaking up organized crime. It has special strike forces in large cities where organized crime is most active. The Criminal Division also handles all criminal matters within the U.S. that affect our safety and security. These are called internal security matters, and include terrorism, treason, and espionage.

Land and Natural Resources

The Land and Natural Resources Division has gained attention lately because of the recent concern that we're quickly using up and polluting our lands. The division works closely with the Environmental Protection Agency (EPA) in settling lawsuits on environmental issues. These include issues like air and water pollution. The division also works to preserve wetlands and other scarce natural resources.

In many cases of pollution, such as hazardous waste cases, the Land and Natural Resources Division tries to protect the public health and make sure that the polluters, not the public, pay for cleaning up the mess. The division is also responsible for federal court cases involving wildlife laws. Prosecutions focus on major smugglers of and dealers in protected species.

In addition to preserving what's left of our natural resources, the division also is responsible for representing the United States in lawsuits brought against it by Indian tribes. In recent years many tribes have tried to get back ancestral land they say was wrongfully taken from them, in violation of treaties the United States signed years ago. In addition to this responsibility, the division also defends Indian tribes against others who may try to take their land or use it illegally. The division also makes sure they keep their rights to hunt and fish on tribal lands.

Tax

The Tax Division represents the United States in court cases involving our federal tax laws. The division's main client (the people it represents the most) is the Internal Revenue Service, a division of a separate cabinet department called the Treasury Department.

Mostly, these court cases arise because of disputes in the way our tax laws are understood. If a citizen disagrees with how much a certain tax should be, he or she first pays the tax. (Refusal to pay taxes is a federal crime.) But after paying the tax, the angry citizen may try to get a refund by bringing a lawsuit against the United States Government. The Tax Division has lawyers who represent the United States in these cases.

The Tax Division also helps fight crime by filing criminal tax lawsuits against wrongdoers. Sometimes this is the only way to put criminals, especially those involved in organized crime, behind bars. In the 1930s, gangster Al Capone sheltered himself from his crimes extremely well. Other law enforcement divisions could never find enough proof of his involvement to send him to jail. He was finally caught, though, when the government proved that he failed to pay his income taxes.

The Bureaus

In addition to overseeing the various divisions of the Justice Department, the Attorney General also oversees several bureaus. These bureaus are organized to deal specifically with law enforcement, which means they investigate and catch criminals who violate federal laws.

Federal Bureau of Investigation

The Federal Bureau of Investigation (FBI) is probably the best known of the Justice Department's operations. The FBI is basically one huge detective agency. It has the task of tracking down all people who violate federal laws, except in cases specifically assigned to other federal agencies. (For example, the Treasury Department tracks down counterfeiters.) Priority has been

assigned to the six areas that affect society the most…organized crime, drugs, counterterrorism, white-collar crime, foreign counterintelligence, and violent crime.

The FBI obviously has a big job to do. Not only must it detect the crimes, it must arrest the criminals and find enough evidence to prosecute them in a court of law. The bureau investigates espionage, sabotage, kidnapping, bank robbery, civil rights violations, and fraud against the government. It also conducts security clearances.

The FBI has its central office in Washington, D.C., but it has 56 field offices and hundreds of agents all over the country. Most FBI agents are trained at

Below: *FBI agents enter the parking garage level of New York's World Trade Center after a bombing that killed several people and injured hundreds.* Right: *The stricken World Trade Center shortly after the bombing.* Inset: *The crater formed by the huge bomb detonated in the underground parking garage.*

the FBI Academy in Quantico, VA. The bureau has incredibly advanced laboratories used in crime detection, and keeps extensive records on known criminals, including a huge library of fingerprint files.

Created in 1908, the FBI greatly increased its influence and functions under director of J. Edgar Hoover. In the 1930s the bureau was widely popular because of its fight against criminal desperadoes like John Dillinger and Baby Face Nelson. FBI agents, because they worked for the U.S. Government, came to be known as "G-Men." (Today many women are agents as well.) During World War II the FBI was very effective in stopping espionage and saboteur plots, as well as capturing criminals who wanted to hurt Americans on our own soil.

During Hoover's controversial final years, the FBI came under attack for what many considered political bias and violation of the constitutional rights of citizens. Today the bureau is more tightly controlled by Congress. It tries to make sure that the FBI sticks with its noble mission of protecting the citizens from criminals and bringing them to justice.

The FBI's controversial Director J. Edgar Hoover.

Bureau of Prisons

When a person is convicted (found guilty) of a federal crime, he or she is taken into custody by the Justice Department's Bureau of Prisons. The bureau is in charge of all federal prisons, called penitentiaries. (When people say, "He was sent to the pen," they're referring to a federal penitentiary.)

Federal prisons are divided into three security classes: maximum, medium, and minimum security. This is because it is important to segregate, or keep separate, hardened criminals from those whose crimes are less severe. If a criminal is a repeat offender who is violent, he or she might be sent to a maximum security prison. If a person commits a crime that has no direct physical harm to citizens, like people who commit white-collar crimes, he or she would usually be sent to a medium or minimum security prison.

In all three types of prisons, inmates are given the chance to get psychiatric help and other counseling. The prisons also run schools and vocational classes. (In many cases offenders are driven to crime because of a lack of education.) The point is to try to rehabilitate prisoners so that they will become law-abiding citizens.

United States Marshals Service

The United States Marshals Service dates back to the
days of George Washington. It is the nation's oldest
Federal law enforcement agency, serving as a
link between the executive and judicial
branches of the government since 1789.

Most people think of the Wild West when they think of
U.S. marshals, with real-life characters like Wild Bill
Hickok or Wyatt Earp restoring law and order to the west-
ern territories. Today's U.S. marshals perform quite different duties. They are mainly responsible for the safety and
physical security of judges, lawyers, juries, and witnesses in all federal
courts.

Marshals also have several other important duties. They are responsible for
catching most Federal fugitives. They maintain custody of and transport
thousands of Federal prisoners each year. They serve court orders and arrest
warrants. They operate the Federal Witness Security program, which makes
sure that government witnesses are protected from harm. Marshals also have
a Special Operations Group, which restores order in riots and mob-violence
situations.

Immigration and Naturalization Service

The Immigration and Naturalization Service (INS) was created in 1891. At first the service was within the Department of Labor, because the first laws to limit immigrants into America were designed to protect workers already here. Immigration laws protected American workers by limiting the number of new workers allowed into the country. With the rise in Communism during the first part of this century, however, lawmakers became less concerned with the number of immigrants allowed in than with what kind of immigrants to let in. The world was deeply divided between the free world and Communist countries. Citizens here were nervous about letting any new people in who might try to harm our way of life by making America a Communist country. For that reason, the Immigration and Naturalization Service was moved to the Justice Department, since it is responsible for protecting the internal security of the United States.

Today the Immigration and Naturalization Service has several duties. It helps people from other countries who want to enter the United States as visitors or immigrants. It works to prevent people from illegally entering the country. It does this by patrolling our border with Canada and Mexico. It also works with the Coast Guard to prevent illegal entry from the ocean. The INS also works to track down people who have managed to slip through illegally and send them back to their home countries.

Drug Enforcement Administration

The Drug Enforcement Administration (DEA) is the top Federal agency in enforcing narcotics and controlled substances laws and regulations. It was created in 1973 by the merger of four separate drug law enforcement agencies. Because of the frightening growth of illegal traffic in narcotics recently, the government needs a single, well-coordinated agency to attack the problem.

The DEA has many well-armed agents who work closely with state and local police to track down and arrest drug dealers. It also works with Interpol, a police force that works all over the world. The DEA's main mission is to shut down drug trafficking operations run by major, well-organized groups like the Mafia or international drug syndicates. The DEA has offices throughout the United States and in 48 foreign countries.

Well-armed DEA agents guard a huge shipment of cocaine seized in Miami, Florida. The cocaine was hidden in concrete fence posts.

Biography: Janet Reno

At the beginning of 1993, newly elected President Clinton was having trouble filling the job of Attorney General. His first choice, corporate lawyer Zoë Baird, was forced to withdraw because it was discovered she violated immigration and tax laws in hiring illegal immigrants. Clinton was ready to nominate federal judge Kimba Wood when he discovered that she too had employed an illegal immigrant to take care of her child. Some people were starting to call these problems "Nannygate." What's a President to do?

Clinton took a hard look at a candidate he had twice passed up: Miami prosecutor Janet Reno. "The one reason that I did not pursue this more was because Janet Reno had always been a state prosecutor and not a federal

Janet Reno being sworn in as America's first woman Attorney General. Also shown are President Bill Clinton, Supreme Court Justice Byron White, and Ms. Reno's niece, who held the bible during the ceremony.

U.S. attorney or not a higher Justice Department official," the President said, explaining why Reno had been overlooked before. "But the more I dug into it and the more I talked to people about it, I realized that you couldn't be the state's attorney in Dade County for 15 years without having enormous exposure to a wide range of issues that the Justice Department deals with." Clinton decided Reno was just the sort of person, socially liberal yet tough with hardened repeat criminals, who could bring confidence back to the Justice Department. The President called to give her the news. Reno told the Miami Herald newspaper, "He didn't really say, 'Do you want it?' It was just, 'Well, are you ready to go?'" Reno was ready to go, and accepted the President's offer, thus becoming the nation's first woman Attorney General.

Dade County, where Miami is located, is one of the country's most crime-ridden areas. As Dade County's head prosecutor, Reno managed an office that employed 900 workers and handled more than 40,000 felony cases each year. Reno had proven herself to be tough on drug dealers, organized crime and corruption. And yet, at the same time, she organized innovative programs for young offenders, giving them a chance at rehabilitation. She thinks the United States needs to spend more money on children's programs to prevent future crime.

Reno's integrity ranks high. James Green of the Florida ACLU said of her, "Janet Reno is as pure as the driven snow." Reno is so law-abiding she had her driver put quarters in the meter even when she parked for Dade County business. And she certainly didn't have the troubles of Clinton's two previous candidates. Reno is not married and has no children. As she says, "I've never hired an illegal alien, and I think I've paid all my Social Security taxes." Asked whether she thinks she got the Attorney General's job simply because she was a woman, Reno replied, "I'm just delighted to be here, and I'm going to try my level best."

Friends and people who have worked with Reno in Florida say she will bring a tough, no-nonsense atmosphere to the Justice Department. She is a

Attorney General Janet Reno.

workaholic who's been known to bring a sleeping bag to the office. She is well known for vigorously going after fathers who refuse to pay child support, and for prosecuting spouse- and child-abuse cases. This has gained her much support from women's groups. When asked if she considers herself a

Attorney General Reno greeting children in a Washington, D.C. school. Ms. Reno is well known for her support of programs that give kids a helping hand by fostering their self respect.

feminist, Reno said, "My mother always told me to do my best, to think my best, and to do right, and to consider myself a person."

Reno was born and raised in Miami. Her father was a police reporter for 40 years at the *Miami Herald*. Her mother was a writer as well, and was also something of a character. She built the family's house not far from the Everglades, and wrestled alligators. Both her parents are now dead, but Reno still lives in the house her mother built.

Reno got her law degree from Harvard Law School in 1963. Before working as a state attorney, she became a partner in a well-respected Miami law firm. In 1979 she was elected Dade County's chief prosecutor. Her start was a rocky one. Her first years in office were marked by racial tensions involving the Miami police force. But Reno worked hard to gain good relations with the black and Hispanic communities in Miami. One time she even marched through a riot-scarred neighborhood trailing an eight-piece Boy Scout band. Her efforts paid off: She was reelected four straight times for her job.

As Attorney General, it will be Reno's job to bring confidence back to a Justice Department that found itself adrift toward the end of the Reagan-Bush years. Many say the Department had become too tied to the President, making legal decisions based on politics instead of law. One of Reno's first actions was to ask for the resignations of U.S. Attorneys in every district in the country. Her goal is to wipe the slate clean, to bring a sense of pride and integrity back to the Justice Department.

Reno's policy goals, how she plans to direct the Justice Department, reflect her background. She'll be putting a high priority on preventing young people from entering the criminal justice system. In Dade County she began a new program that set up a drug court. This program sent nonviolent, first-time offenders (many of whom are young people under age 18) to counseling rather than to jail. Reno believes that building kid's self respect and giving them a helping hand is better than throwing them in jail, which she says only makes them tougher criminals. She supports sending young offenders to work projects in order to instill discipline. Her goal is to reach kids at an early age to prevent crime from happening over and over again.

Reno will also pay special attention to environmental protection and civil rights, which reflects her liberal roots. But at the same time, she can be as tough as nails, showing little patience with violent repeat offenders. Reno shows no hesitation at throwing the book at habitual criminals. As President Clinton said of her, "She has lived the kind of life in real contact with the toughest problems of this country that I think will serve her very well as the nation's chief law enforcement officer."

The Attorney General's job can sometimes be a thankless one. Many problems develop into no-win situations, and tough decisions have to be made. In the spring of 1993 Janet Reno made a decision that turned out to be disastrously wrong. The Branch Davidian cult standoff in Waco, Texas, had dragged on for 51 days. The cult's leader, David Koresh, and his approximately 95 followers showed no sign of ever giving up. Reports were coming in that the children held in the cult's compound were being abused. The FBI came to Reno with a plan to pump tear gas into the buildings with the hope that the cultists would finally give up. Reno agonized over the safety of the children, fearing a mass suicide by the cultists. She finally decided that suicide was unlikely. She got approval from President Clinton, then gave her okay for the FBI to go ahead with the assault. But instead of fleeing, the cultists set the entire compound ablaze in a mass suicide, just as authorities had feared. Fanned by strong winds, the wooden buildings quickly turned into an inferno, killing over 80 cult members. Less than 10 survived. Ironically, none of the children made it out alive. Asked about her decision, Reno said, "Based on what we know now, it was obviously wrong." She called it, "the hardest decision in the world to make." Although Reno and President Clinton took full responsibility for the assault, the deaths of the cult members, including more than 17 children, lie solely in the hands of cult leader David Koresh. Still, the inferno in Waco will haunt Janet Reno's memories for the rest of her life. The Attorney General's job is not an easy one.

Far Left: *The Branch Davidian compound near Waco, Texas, goes up in flames after the cultists apparently committed mass suicide by fire.*
Left: *Attorney General Reno, during a news conference shortly after the fire, took full responsibility for the raid. "I am accountable, the buck stops with me."*

Glossary

Cabinet

A body of persons appointed by a chief of state or a prime minister to head the executive departments of the government and to act as his or her official advisers.

Civil Law

Civil law is law dealing with relationships between people, as opposed to criminal law, which deals with offenses against the state, or government. If somebody sued a neighbor because of a dispute over property lines, for example, it would be a civil case. If the neighbor lost his case, got mad, and ran over his neighbor with his car, it would be a criminal case.

Congress

The national legislative body of the United States, consisting of the Senate and the House of Representatives. This is the place where laws get made.

Constitution

The system of laws and principles that guide countries on the nature and limits of government. The U.S. Constitution took effect in 1789. It establishes a federal republic with power balanced between the national government and the states. Within the national government, power is separated among three branches: the Executive (President), legislative (Congress), and judicial (Supreme Court). The U.S. Constitution is the supreme law of the land; no other law, state constitution or statute, federal legislation, or executive order can operate in conflict with it.

Counterfeiter

A person who makes fake money, usually with the intent to steal.

Criminal Law

This is the kind of law that defines offenses against the state, or government. They include things like murder, kidnapping, theft, drug dealing, fraud, treason, etc. The procedure in criminal cases is pretty much the same throughout the U.S. First, a Grand Jury looks at evidence that's been found against a suspect. If the Grand Jury thinks enough evidence has been found (this is called probable cause), then it issues an indictment, which means the case goes to court. Trials can be either by jury or by a judge alone. At this point, the suspect is still presumed innocent. It is up to the prosecution to prove beyond a reasonable doubt that the suspect is guilty.

Supreme Court

The Supreme Court is the highest court of the United States. It has the final say in all court cases arising under the Constitution, laws, and treaties of the U.S. The Supreme Court makes its decisions by majority vote. It has nine members, a chief justice and eight associate justices. Each member is appointed by the president, but must be confirmed by the Senate. Justices keep their jobs for life. In addition to being the highest court in the land, it has two other important functions of last resort: interpreting acts of Congress and deciding whether federal and state laws conform to the Constitution.

Watergate

The Watergate affair was a series of scandals involving President Richard Nixon. In July 1972 agents of Nixon's reelection committee were arrested in Democratic party headquarters, in the Watergate apartment building in Washington, D.C., after an attempt to tap telephones there. They were tried and convicted in 1973, but the case didn't end there. People suspected that officials higher up in the government knew about the break-in and were trying to cover it up.

Special Senate committees were formed to look into these suspicions. During one of the committee meetings John Dean, the former White House counsel, said that members of the Nixon administration, notably Attorney General John Mitchell, had known of the Watergate burglary. The scandal grew when the committee found out that Nixon had secretly taped conversations in his office in the White House. A special prosecutor, Archibald Cox, tried to get copies of the tapes, but was fired by Nixon. Cox's replacement, Leon Jaworski, did manage to get copies of the tapes. They uncovered widespread evidence of political espionage by the Nixon reelection committee, illegal wiretapping of citizens by the administration, and corporate contributions to the Republican party in return for political favors. Jaworski convicted several Nixon Administration officials, including Dean and Mitchell.

In the meantime, public confidence in the President and the Justice Department had reached a new low. In July of 1974 Congress began the process of impeaching President Nixon, which means trying to remove him from office. But on August 9, 1974, before they could forcibly remove him, Nixon resigned, the first time a U.S. President had ever done so. One month later, his successor, Gerald Ford, pardoned Nixon, saying that America needed to put the past behind it and get on with running the country.

White Collar Crime

White-collar crime refers to crimes committed by corporations or individuals in the course of their business activities. These crimes include theft, false advertising, unfair competition, tax evasion, and unfair labor practices. (It's called white collar crime because so many business people wear white shirts under their suits.)

Connect With Books

Acheson, Patrician C. *Our Federal Government: How It Works*. New York: Dodd, Mead & Company, 1984.

Boot, Max. "Justice Nominee Reno Offers New Priorities." *The Christian Science Monitor*, February 18, 1993, p. 8.

Cunliffe, Marcus. *The American Heritage History of the Presidency*. American Heritage Publishing Company, 1968.

DeGregorio, William A. *The Complete Book of U.S. Presidents*. New York: Dembner Books, 1984.

Gest, Ted. "Democrats' Chance to Attack Crime." *U.S. News & World Report*, February 22, 1993, pp. 28-29.

Gilfond, Henry. *The Executive Branch of the United States Government*. New York: Franklin Watts, 1981.

Howe, John R. *From Revolution Through the Age of Jackson*. Englewood Cliffs, New Jersey: Prentice-Hall, Inc., 1973.

Kaplan, David. "Janet Reno: 'Are You Ready to Go?'" *Newsweek*, February 22, 1993, pp. 26-27.

Parker, Nancy Winslow. *The President's Cabinet and How It Grew*. HarperCollins Publishers, 1991.

"Reno Named Attorney General." *Minneapolis Star Tribune*, February 12, 1992, p. 1A.

Sullivan, George. *How the White House Really Works*. New York: Scholastic, 1990.

The United States Government Manual 1991/1992. Washington, D.C.: Office of the Federal Register, 1991.

Watson, Richard. *Promise & Performance of American Democracy*. New York: John Wiley & Sons, Inc., 1978.

Index

Antitrust Division 11
Baird, Zoë 7–8, 21
Branch Davidian compound raid 26–27
Capone, Al 14
Civil Division 12
Civil Rights Division 12
Clinton, Bill 5, 7, 21–22, 26
Criminal Division 12–13
Dillinger, John 16
Drug Enforcement Adminstration 20
Environmental Protection Agency 13
Federal Bureau of Investigation 14–16, 27
Federal law 6
Ford, Gerald 7
Hoover, J. Edgar 16
Immigration and Nuturalization Service 19
Internal Revenue Service 13
Judiciary Act of 1789 8
King, Rodney 12
Land and Natural Resources Division 13
Levi, Edward 7
Marshals Service, United States 18
Nelson, Baby Face 16
Nixon, Richard 7
Prisons, Bureau of 17
Randolph, Edmund Jennings 8–9
Reno, Janet 21–27
Tax Division 13–14
Treasury Department 14
Trust busting 11
Washington, George 8
White, Byron 21
Wood, Kimba 21
World Trade Center bombing 15